How I Learned to Cook

Great Creole Food

Gaylord Boyd

How I Learned to Cook Great Creole Food
Copyright © 2025 — Raphael Gaylord Boyd
All rights reserved under United States, Pan American, and
International copyright conventions.

Published by:

A Father, Two Sons and a Daughter Publications
916 Mayflower Street
Baton Rouge, LA 70802-6322

ISBN: 978-1-964665-26-9

Printed on demand in the U.S., the U.K, and Australia
For Worldwide Distribution

FROM GRAM, POP, and
A HOST OF FAMILY MEMBERS AND FRIENDS

A collection of good Creole recipes and important facts about the Creole people and their unique heritage, as well as customs that were passed on from one generation to another

A Father, Two Sons and a Daughter Publication

"If we know more about the past, we can appreciate the present and strengthen our faith in the future"

T. M ALEXANDER, SR.

To:

Raphael II, Ezra Joseph, and Eman, and my parents, Joseph Raphael and Stella Hebert Boyd. To the members of the Boyd and Hebert families, living and dead, who have made a great contribution to the preservation of a rich family heritage. To all the chefs, and cooks and those I've watched through the years who have invented, developed, disseminated, and preserved an art—the art of cooking. To those who have continued to keep the Creole heritage alive for generations, to share with future generations.

I hope you will enjoy the many hours I've spent learning, experiencing, and preparing these recipes.

Design & Layout Compliments to J-Rome

Table of Contents

Chapter 1	The Herb Garden	8
Chapter 2	Good Things To Drink	10
Chapter 3	Let's Start Something: Appetizers	13
Chapter 4	Soups	18
Chapter 5	Sauces: Let's Sauce It Up!	20
Chapter 6	Great Salads and Good Dressings	23
Chapter 7	Good Creole Vegetables	26
Chapter 8	Breads: Let's Bake Creole Style	32
Chapter 9	Creole Bar-B-Que	36
Chapter 10	Gumbo	41
Chapter 11	On With the Seafood!	43
Chapter 12	Crabs, Crabs, and More Crabs	46
Chapter 13	Eat Oysters; Live Longer	48
Chapter 14	Oh Boy! Crawfish!	49
Chapter 15	Creole Sweet Treats	51
Chapter 16	A Host of Friends	58

INTRODUCTION

The term *Creole* is used to define, in Louisiana, a person of the Black race who was born in one of the former new-world possessions of France, Spain, or Portugal and whose ancestors came originally from one or more of these countries. The word is from the French *creole*, which is, more or less, the equivalent of the Spanish word *criollo*. The majority opinion holds Creoles to be of Hispanic origin, deriving from the Spanish verb *crear*, to create, to give birth to. Another school of thought claims it stems from Portuguese. The latter holds that Criollo was adopted from the Portuguese word meaning a slave born in the master's household and is derived from the Portuguese verb *criar*, to give birth.

There is a widespread belief that Creole refers to a person who has a mixture of Negro and European blood. In Louisiana, Creole refers to persons who have a mixture of Negro blood.

The Louisiana, Creoles were descendants from the French and Spanish. The close cultural bond between the Louisiana Creole and France continued until the Civil War. The contemporary Creoles of Louisiana are fully integrated into the life of the United States, but are still mainly found in Southern Louisiana. The Creoles overcame many obstacles and were able to keep alive their traditions and cultural heritage. This continues to happen with many young Creoles who strive to keep alive their Creole heritage.

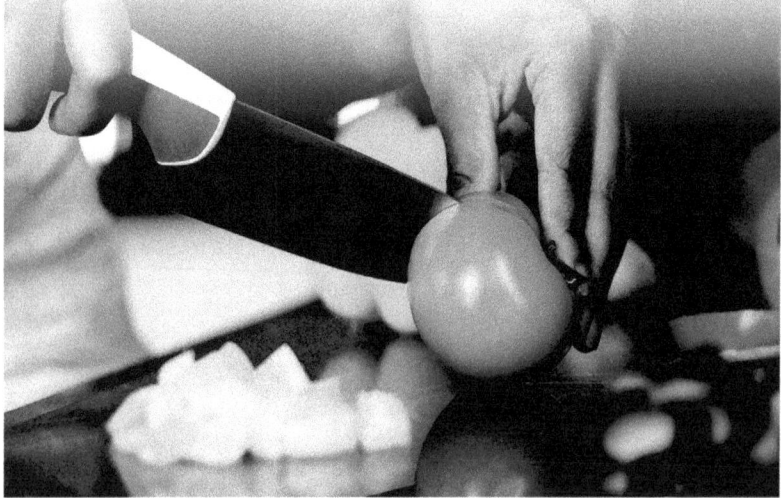

WELCOME TO "A CULINARY ADVENTURE"

A recipe is something that's made up of a lot of ingredients and measurements, a little of this and a little of that. What I've done here is to take these family recipes and apply a little magic to each of them so that they're no longer just written words on paper but have been transformed into something you'll be proud to cook for yourself and your family members.

As we all know, Creole cooking is a mixture, the result of the many you contributed to the great variety of foods we now experience. These include the French, the Spanish, the Native American Indians, Blacks or African-Americans, and a vast number of representatives from the islands of the West Indies and the Caribbean. The Blacks or Africans-Americans have made the greatest contribution to the art of Creole cooking and have also helped to preserve it and prove it a noteworthy art. These Blacks or African-Americans spent many hours in the kitchen doing it the way they were taught to do it, making a rue very dark and brown, burning the onions but not too much, just enough to bring out the flavor. These, like our early ancestors, have struggled to keep Creole cooking alive enough to survive through many generations.

Many tourists from around the U.S. and the world travel to the nooks and crannies of the 64 parishes of Louisiana just to experience the total magic of Creole cooking. It is this magic that makes the food taste so good, better than anything I've ever experienced in my life. This cookbook will help you uncover the magic of a great cuisine that is sometimes difficult. The rules of the game will be written in the rule book (this cookbook), and you'll find that once you read the rules, you'll know how to play the game and be satisfied with the results. — Chef R. Gaylord Boyd

THE HERB GARDEN
Spice/Herb Tips/Creole Seasonings & Rubs

The herb garden entered into every aspect of Creole life. Not only did it provide medicines, but also numerous beverages. Not only were traditional spices used in the Creole culture, but local inhabitants provided specialties. The Choctaw Indians shared a great secret with the Creoles. The Creoles learned of file'–dried and powdered sassafras leaves. It was used by the Creoles in their preparation of stews, soups, and gumbo. Herbs are also used in court bouillon, bouillabaisse, and jambalaya. The Creoles knew that many of the dishes prepared had to have some type of herb or spice to make it taste just right.

> The older Creoles of my mother and grandmother's generation always used and kept available a bouquet-garnish. A bouquet-garnish consist of 1 or 2 sprigs of parsley, 1 of thyme, 1 or 2 pieces of celery, a bay leaf or two, all tied together with a piece of string.

In Southern Louisiana, Creole country, herbs were grown very easily because of the climate. The herbs the Creoles grew were sage, rosemary, thyme, basil, anise, dill, mint, tarragon, and fennel.

All Creoles had an herb garden and in some cultures, the Creoles would swap herbs and spices with other Creoles. The herbs were always gathered right at peak growth, washed and then tied or hung so they could dry. The Creoles also knew they needed enough herbs and spices to last through the winter.

The use of herbs and spices, to the Creoles, was like that of enjoying a fine painting. The success or failure of a roux-based Creole dish depended to a great extent on how those herbs and spices were used. "Season to taste" was the Creole motto. If you execut-ed this well, you were classified as a true Creole cook.

SPICE/HERB TIPS

Keep your herb and spice containers tightly covered to hold in the flavor. To judge the strength of your herbs or spices, crush a little in your hand, rub a bit, then sniff.

Cook with one herb or spice at a time so you can learn the characteristics. Measure your herbs and spices lightly because their flavor builds.

When preparing stews, soups, and sauces, add your herbs/spices in the last hour of cook-ing. Always try to obtain fresh herbs/spices when you can. Fresh always adds an extra flavor to your dishes.

CREOLE SEASONING/RUB BASIC SEASONING

4 tbsp black pepper
3 tbsp salt
2 tbsp white pepper
2 tbsp cayenne pepper
2 tbsp paprika
2 tbsp granulated garlic
1 tbsp ground cumin

BASIC RUB

3 tbsp salt
4 tbsp white pepper
4 tbsp chili powder
2 tbsp cayenne pepper
2 tbsp paprika
4 tbsp accent
2 tbsp garlic powder
3 tbsp onion powder

ONION RING SEASONING

1/2 cups all-purpose flour
3 to 5 heaping tsps corn meal
3 tbsp onion powder
2 tsps salt or accent
2 Tbsp cayenne & black pepper
1 Tbsp lemon pepper

Combine the above dry ingredients with the following:

Wet ingredients to make batter:
1 1/2 cup milk, Half & Half or heavy cream
1 egg (large or jumbo)
1/2 cup water

How I Learned to Cook Great Creole Food

GOOD THINGS TO DRINK

The Creole people take pride in the beverages they love to serve and drink. Their inherited drinking tastes are so vast that I take this time to share the abundance of all these great beverages from A to Z.

At dinners in Creole homes, wine was served with many of the meals. The Creole culture took pride in making wines, liqueurs and cordials. These were guarded recipes, only transferred from family to family.

The favorites included anisette, crème de mint, wine punches, brandy, sherry, juleps, sangrias, toddies (hot or cold), crèmes, and beer. I hope you prepare some of my family's great beverages to satisfy your thirst.

So, on with the great beverages of the Creoles....

COFFEE

The Creole culture has always made coffee a part of any event. To the Creole coffee was worth drinking. Just remember the old-fashioned way to make coffee in the Creole home was the "drip method." The dark, rich flavor of the coffee added the gourmet touch Creoles gave to entertaining. A great coffee always reflected the hospitality and graciousness of the host. So serve good coffee: internationals, chicory, and good rich, dark roast.

(I.E.'S CHRISTINE PAUL'S) ANISETTE

6 to 7 1/2 ounces alcohol
5 to 7 drops oil of anise
Simple syrup - sufficient quantity for 1 to 3 1/2 quarts
2 or 4 slices of lemon
Bring water to boil. Add sugar, dissolve and let cool.

POP'S SIMPLE SYRUP
(JOSEPH RAPHAEL BOYD'S RECIPE)

1 cup water
1 cup sugar (white or brown)

Pour water in small saucepan. Add sugar. Stir until sugar is dissolved.

NAN CORINE - CORINE JACKSON'S EGG NOG

1 quart milk
4 eggs (separated)
1/2 cup sugar ¼ tsp nutmeg
Good whiskey (or any brandy)

Scald the milk. Beat egg yolks and sugar until creamy. Add a small amount of scalded milk to egg mixture and stir well. Combine egg mixture with remaining milk. Stir and cook on low heat until thoroughly blended. Beat egg whites until stiff and fold in. Add nutmeg and whiskey to taste.

ALPHONSE JACKSON'S
Uncle Al's Gin Fizz

1 1/2 tsps lemon juice
2 tsp sugar (regular or brown)
3 drops orange flavor or (orange flavor water)
2 drop vanilla extract
1 jigger gin (good expensive gin)
1 jigger of heavy cream in crushed ice. Shake well and serve.

WILLIAM BOYD SR., PA - PA'S
Holiday Punch

2 cups muscatel wine
1/4 cup kummel
1/2 cup dry vermouth
1 piece of cinnamon stick
2 cloves
1/4 lemon
1/2 cup sugar
Handful of raisins
2 cardamom seeds

Put all ingredients overnight in a china pitcher and let stand. Use the next day cold over ice or heat (warm).

VIRGINIA BOYD'S YELLOW NEW ORLEANS

1 jigger crème de banana
1 jigger rum (86 or 151 proof)
1 dash lemon
1 dash pineapple juice
1 dash orange juice

Put the mixture in a blender with crushed ice. Pour into a martini glass and top with a slice of lemon.

PA-REE FELIX HEBERT JR.'S
Mint Julep

3 sprigs mint
3 ounces Bourbon (coal oil, that's what Pa-Ree called bourbon)
1/2 ounce of J. R. Boyd's simple syrup
Crushed ice

Crush 3 sprigs of mint in a tall glass. Add JR's simple syrup and bourbon and crushed mint. Fill glass with crushed ice. Garnish with a sprig of mint and serve when glasses are well frosted.

GLORIA G. HEBERT
Auntie Glo's Hot Punch - Punch for the Kids

1 large bottle or can apple juice
2-3 lemon slices
2 sticks cinnamon
1/2 tbsp cloves

Simmer for 3 or 4 minutes. Serve hot with mint.

CORA LEE HEBERT FIGARO
(Nina)
Peach Daiquiri

3 ripe peaches
1 can frozen pink lemonade or frozen limeade
1 tsp sugar
1 ½ cup white rum
1 tray of ice cubes

Blend for 10 seconds. Serve in sherbet glass with a short straw.

LET'S START SOMETHING
APPETIZERS

In the Creole days, you invited guests to share a great evening at your home. Before dinner you took pride in serving a little appetizer. To make it simple, appetizers are and were known as little bits or starters. These appetizers are called the first course, the beginning before the end.

STUFFED CELERY
(AUNTIE' NORA STYLE)
Elenora Figaro Hebert, Celery Treats

1 4 oz. cream cheese
2 tsps mayonnaise
1/2 cup finely chopped pecans & almonds.
1/4 tsp Worcestershire sauce
2 large stalks celery
Cayenne pepper

Cream together the cream cheese, mayonnaise, Worcestershire sauce, and cayenne pep-per. Add almonds and pecans. Clean and string celery before stuffing, using only inner, tender ribs. This will stuff 2 large stalks of celery. Sprinkle with accent, lemon pepper, and cayenne pepper.

GAYLORD'S QUICK ONION DIP

1 carton of sour cream
2 packages of Lipton Onion Soup Mix

Mix both ingredients together in bowl. Refrigerate after mixing 2 to 3 hours or longer. When ready to serve, pour in serving bowl.

UNCLE BILL'S (WILLIAM BOYD, JR.)
Stuffed Mushrooms

12 fresh mushrooms
1 cup fresh lump crab meat
2 tbsp butter
1/2 cup hollandaise sauce
3 tbsp whipping cream
2 tsps sour cream

Poach and dry mushrooms on paper towel. Combine remaining ingredients. Heat and stir until fluffy. You can stuff each mushroom individually with mixture. Broil together until lightly browned in 350° oven.

SHRIMP DIP

1 to 1 1/2 lb. fresh boiled seasoned shrimp
1 medium onion, grated
3 8oz. cream cheese
2 cloves minced garlic
2 tbsp Worcestershire sauce
1 tbsp chopped parsley (fresh if possible)
Juice of one lemon
Red pepper and salt to taste

Mix all ingredients, except boiled shrimp. Beat until fluffy. Add shrimp. Serve with warm crushed taco shells or corn chips.

HORS D'OEUVRES

For spur of the moment occasions and for your own snacking, keep a few of these canned or packaged appetizers on hand: Cheese spreads in a variety of flavors, cheese wedges, chunks, or slices, potato chips, boned chicken or turkey, pretzels, tuna, onion-flavored crackers, Melba toast, crisp rye crackers, dill & sweet pickles, corn chips, shredded wheat wafers, popcorn, chicken-flavored crackers, salted nuts, olives, luncheon meat: chopped ham, deviled ham, chicken, liverwurst, sesame crackers, cocktail sausage and cheese crackers.

MARLENE'S QUICK CHEESE DIP

1 8 oz. carton of sour cream
2 tbsp crumbled blue cheese
1/2 cup minced onion
Chopped fresh parsley

Combine sour cream, blue cheese, onion and a dash of salt in mixing bowl. Cover and refrigerate. When ready to serve, garnish with chopped parsley.

MILDRED HEBERT BIRD (TaTe')
Catfish Nuggets (Makes 6 dozen)

1 cup finely crushed cheese crackers
6 catfish fillets
1/2 cup grated Parmesan cheese
1/4 cup sesame seeds
1/2 tsp salt
1/4 tsp black pepper
1/2 cup butter or margarine (melted)
(Sour cream blue cheese dip)

Cut fillets into 1 inch cubes and set aside. Combine cracker crumbs, Parmesan cheese, sesame seeds, and salt and pepper in a small bowl. Dip fish cubes in melted butter. Roll in cracker crumb mixture. Place fish cubes 1 inch apart on a baking sheet. Bake uncovered in preheated 400° oven for 20 minutes or until golden brown. Serve immediately with blue cheese dip, flavored bar-b-que sauce or catsup.

GAYLORD'S CREOLE SWEDISH MEATBALLS

¾ lb ground beef
½ lb ground veal
¼ lb ground pork
1 ½ cup bread crumbs (plain or seasoned)
1 cup half and half or light cream
½ cup chopped onion
1 egg
3 tbsp butter
¼ cup minced parsley
1 ½ tsp salt
¼ tsp ginger
Dash of pepper and nutmeg

Soak bread crumbs in cream for 5 to 7 minutes. Saute' onions in 1 tbsp butter. Combine all ingredients and mix for 5 to 6 minutes on medium speed in electric mixer. Stop mixer and mix ingredients by hand for 10 minutes. Use a small ice cream scoop to form 1 inch meatballs. Place 1 inch balls in iron skillet with 2 tbsp of butter. When meatballs are brown place on paper towel covered baking sheet to drain. Use bar-b-que sauce or make flavored catsup with Worcestershire sauce, garlic, and onion.

JOHN WESLEY BOYD
Uncle Wesley

Crab Cocktail (Serves 8)
2 cups canned or fresh crab meat
1 tbsp seasoned mayonnaise
Juice of two limes
Salt to taste
Coarsely ground black pepper
1 tsp chopped fresh tarragon or parsley or both

Mix crab meat with just enough mayonnaise to moisten. Add lime juice, salt and pepper and mix well. Spoon crab mixture into small glass cups. Set in crushed ice. Sprinkle chopped tarragon or parsley over each cocktail and serve.

LAWRENCE BOYD
Uncle Larry's Hot Pepper Pecans

Preheat oven to 300°F 1 8 or 9 inch cake pan

Combine 2 cups pecan with 1 1/2 tbsp melted butter. Toast in oven 30 minutes, stirring occasionally. Add 1 tsp salt, 2 tsps soy sauce, and 1/8 tsp hot pepper sauce. Toss. Makes 2 cups.

GEORGE LESTER BOYD
Uncle George Hot Bacon Bites

Wrap half a bacon slice around one of the following (below. Skewer with toothpick and broil until bacon is crisp, turning once or twice. (You can also do this on the grill.

Pineapple chunks, shelled and de-veined shrimp, canned pear chunks, chicken livers, raw oysters, luncheon meat or ham cubes, or cocktail franks.

BERTHA D. BOYD
Auntie Bea's Swiss Cheese-Pepper Squares

3 wheat or white bread slices (Roman meal, cut)
1/4 lb. Swiss cheese, cut in short thin strips
1/2 small green pepper, cut in short thin strips (regular peppers or you can use red or golden peppers, mild or hot)
1/4 cup mayonnaise
dash salt

Trim crust from bread slices with each into 4 squares. In a small bowl, combine remaining ingredients. Pile mixture on to bread. Cover and refrigerate. (Makes 12 appetizers.

LINDA HEBERT DAIGRE
Linda Crab Salad

2- 7 ½ ounce can crabs or fresh crabs.
1/2 cup mayonnaise
1/3 cup minced celery
1 tsp lemon juice
¼ tsp pepper
24 boiled shrimp
2 package of 12 baked small dinner rolls
3 small heads of lettuce (your choice)
Salad dressing (your choice)

In medium bowl, flake crab. Stir in mayonnaise, celery, lemon juice, and pepper. Cut dinner rolls in half. On each half, place small lettuce leaf. Top with crab mixture. Add your choice of salad dressing. Garnish with boiled shrimp.

SIDNEY JOSEPH BOYD
Uncle Sidney's Guacamole Creole Style

1 medium avocado, cut up,
1 medium tomato, cut up
1 hot pepper (your choice)
1/2 small onion chopped
2 tbsp lemon juice
1 tsp seasoned salt
1/4 tsp hot pepper sauce (your choice)

In a covered blender at low speed, blend all ingredients until smooth. (Makes 1 3/4 cups). Dip with potato chips, com chips, crackers, or heated crushed taco shells and salsa.

SOUP

Soup is truly the signature of the Creole cuisine. A morning cup of bouillon was served with breakfast and then later relegated to later meals.

Here is a collection of great soups you can serve anytime. Just remember, soups come in a wide variety of choices: condensed, ready to serve, dry, mixed, and condensed broth bases.

Soups that are good served alone take on new interest when combined with other soups. I urge you to create your own specialties by mixing 2 or more kinds or try one of the combinations that I will give you. Just remember, always prepare them according to label directions, combining and heating.

Tomato, Chicken and Rice; Cheddar Cheese and Tomato; Chicken Gumbo and Tomato; Cream of Mushroom, Asparagus, and Cheese; Clam Chowder; Tomato and Fresh Crawfish Tails; Turkey, Chicken, and Cream of Mushroom; and Chili and Tomato.

UNCLE JESSE'S
(JESSE RUSSELL HEBERT) Beef Vegetable Soup

6 to 8 lbs. beef shanks
3 stalks celery, diced
3 large carrots, diced
2 medium onions, diced
1, 8 oz. can of Tomatoes or 4 large fresh tomatoes
1/2 cup parsley chopped
1/2 tsp basil, thyme leaves, and tsp pepper
1 10 oz. pack of each: frozen lima beans, corn, and peas

In a very large kettle, over high heat, heat beef, 2 tbsp salt and 10 cups hot water to boiling. Reduce heat to low. Add remaining ingredients, except for frozen vegetables. Cover and simmer for 2 hours. Add frozen vegetables and 2 tsps salt and c ook 30 minutes or until vegetables are tender. (Makes 26 cups or 4 servings.

JOSEPH RAPHAEL BOYD
Uncle Ray's Corn Soup

3 large onions chopped
3 cans corn or 6 fresh cobs
2 cans water
3 tbsp cooking oil
1 ham bone from baked ham
1 1/2 lbs. canned or fresh tomatoes
Salt and pepper to taste

Place oil in sauce pan and heat. Sauté onions until clear and soft. Add ham or (ham bone. Add a pinch of sugar to tomatoes. Add tomatoes to sauce pan and simmer with onions 5 minutes. Add corn, water, salt and pepper and simmer about 45 minutes. (Serve over flavored croutons.

GAYLORD'S RED BEAN SOUP
(GAYLORD BOYD)

Leftover red beans
1/2 tsp thyme
Few drops Tabasco sauce or pepper sauce of your choice
Water
1 to 2-day-old French bread

Put cooked beans in a blender with enough water to mix. Pour into sauce pan and heat. Add thyme and Tabasco sauce. Cut slices of French bread to use as croutons and serve hot.

CREOLE PEA SOUP
Stella Tee Tee Hebert Boyd's

1/4 cup butter or margarine
2 cups shredded lettuce
1/2 large onion, chopped
1 tbsp all-purpose flour
2 14.5 oz. cans of chicken broth
1 10 oz. pack of frozen or canned peas
1 cup milk
1/4 tsp ground coriander

In a large sauce pan, over medium heat, in hot butter, cook lettuce and onion until tender. Stir often. Slowly add flour and coriander (ground). Slowly stir in broth. Add peas and cook covered for 15 minutes. In blender, blend mixture one cup at a time and return to pot. Add milk. (Makes 8 to 12 cups.)

UNCLE JESSE'S
(JESSE RUSSELL HEBERT) Creole Onion Soup

1 tbsp butter
1 large onion, thinly sliced
2 egg yolks
6 cups milk
2 tsps salt
1/4 tsp mace or nutmeg
Croutons for garnish

In a large skillet, over medium heat, add melted butter or margarine. Cook onions until clear. In large bowl, with fork, beat egg yolks. Stir in milk, salt and mace or nutmeg. Add onions and cook, stirring constantly until soup thickens slightly. Serve sprinkled with croutons. (Makes 6 to 8 servings.)

CREOLE SAUCES
"SAUCE IT UP"!

A sauce is something to cover or accent, something simmered in its own juice, or something added to spice up and add a new delicacy to your cooking.

CREOLE SAUCE

10 soft tomatoes
3 onions chopped
3 ribs chopped celery or leaves from bunch
1 1/2 to 2 chopped green bell peppers (red, gold, or mixed)
1 tbsp oregano
Salt and pepper
Hot sauce to taste
1 tbsp parsley
2 tbsp liquid smoke flavoring

Cook onion in bacon fat until soft. Add tomatoes one at a time, stirring over high heat. Add remaining ingredients and cook 4-5 minutes. This is great for all types of sandwiches and to dress up chicken, hamburgers, and leftovers. Freeze in 1 cup portions.

HOLLANDAISE SAUCE

8 tbsp butter
3 egg yolks
Juice of 1/2 lemon

Melt butter by putting in cup of standing hot water. Put eggs in double boiler over very slow fire. Add lemon juice and mix constantly. When egg yolks and lemon juice are thoroughly blended, remove from flame and very slowly add melted butter, stirring while adding to prevent cracking. If sauce becomes thickened, add a little water and mix.

CREOLE LEMON BUTTER

1/4 cup butter or margarine
1 tbsp lemon juice
1 tbsp chopped parsley
1/2 tsp salt
Dash cayenne pepper

In small sauce pan, over medium heat, melt butter or margarine. Stir in remaining ingredients. Serve hot or over cooked vegetables, boiled, fried, or poached fish or shellfish. (Makes about 1/3 cup.)

SOUR CREAM / CREOLE MUSTARD SAUCE

1 cup sour cream
1 tbsp minced onion
1 tbsp prepared mustard or Creole mustard
1/4 tsp salt dash pepper
1 tsp chopped parsley

In small sauce pan, over very low heat, heat first 5 ingredients just until hot. Sprinkle with parsley. (Makes about 1 cup.)

STEAK SAUCE

6 tbsp Dijon or Creole mustard
6 tbsp Worcestershire sauce
10 tbsp butter
Tabasco sauce to taste

In a small sauce pan, combine mustard, Worcestershire sauce, and butter. Place over low heat, stirring constantly until butter is melted and sauce is hot. DO NOT BOIL! Adjust seasoning with Tabasco. (Makes up to 1 1/3 cups.)

CREOLE BORDELAISE SAUCE

2 tbsp butter or margarine
2 tbsp all-purpose flour
1 tbsp minced onion 1 tbsp minced parsley
1 bay leaf
1/4 tsp thyme leaves
 1/4 tsp salt
¼ cup dry red wine
1/8 tsp coarsely ground pepper
1 10 1/2 oz. can condensed beef broth (bouillon)

In a 1 quart heavy sauce pan, over low heat, in hot butter or margarine, cook flour until lightly brown. Stir in onion, parsley, bay leaf, thyme, salt and pepper. Stir in undiluted beef broth and wine. Increase heat to medium-high and cook mixture, stirring constantly until thickened. Discard bay leaf. Serve hot over roast, steaks, or broiled beef. (Makes about 1 1/3 cups.)

POULTRY BASTING SAUCE

12 tbsp melted butter
2 tsps paprika
1 tsp sugar
1 tsp salt
½ tsp pepper
½ tsp dry mustard
Pinch cayenne pepper
½ cup lemon juice
½ cup hot water
Few drops hot sauce

Combine butter and seasonings. Blend in lemon juice, hot water, and hot sauce. 2 tbsp of grated onion may be added. (Yields 1 1/2 cups.)

GREAT SALADS AND GOOD DRESSINGS

You start with the right greens, throw in garnishes, and you will come up with many taste tempting and delicious salads of the Creoles. Choose from a vast variety of greens. Various lettuces combined with other greens can offer a wide variety in salads that are easy to achieve. The Creoles combined tangy greens with mild-flavored ones, light and dark colored for contrast in flavor, texture, and color. The Creoles knew that greens add good nutrition to your menus

1. They are low in calories
2. They are high in vitamins A & C.
3. They are rich in minerals (iron and calcium).
4. Always shred the leaves, never cut them.

Here are a few helpful tips to prepare the best Creole salads ever:
- When buying, always choose the freshest, crispest looking, and firmest and those that are free from bruises and brown-tipped leaves.
- Clean well. Store in plastic when saving. Choose the right garnishes for your salad like these: bacon bits, ripe, green, or stuffed olives, shredded lemon, lime, or orange peel, maraschino cherries, cocktail onions, pomegranate seeds, carrot (curls, sticks, or shreds), radishes (roses or sliced), sliced or minced eggs, celery curls, parsley, mint, watercress sprigs, chopped nuts, croutons, various cheeses, cherry tomatoes (various types), and stuffed dates.
- Knowing the right combination, you will make the best salads ever. So let's try some of the Creole's favorites.

CREOLE HERBED TOMATO SALAD

6 medium tomatoes (home grown when in season- any variety)
2 tbsp salad oil
1 tsp wine vinegar (red)
1/2 tsp oregano leaves
1/2 tsp salt
1/2 tsp pepper

Slice tomatoes and arrange in serving dish (overlapping slices). In a small bowl, combine remaining ingredients and sprinkle over tomatoes. Cover and refrigerate. Add the lettuce of your choice, if desired. (Serves 6.)

CREOLE DELUXE COLESLAW

1 medium head cabbage, shredded (about 8 cups)
1 small green bell pepper (red or yellow), thinly sliced
2 2/3 cups diced celery
2/3 cup finely shredded carrots
1/2 cup sliced radishes
3 tbsp minced onions

In large bowl, gently toss all ingredients. Cover and refrigerate. (Serves 8)

Dressing:

1/2 cup mayonnaise
1 tbsp milk
1 tbsp vinegar or lemon juice
1/2 tsp sugar
1/4 tsp salt
Dash paprika and pepper

In a cup, stir all ingredients until well blended. Cover and refrigerate. Combine dressing with Creole coleslaw mixture. (Makes 1/2 cup.)

OLD FASHIONED CREOLE LETTUCE SALAD

1 cup Half and Half
1/2 cup vinegar
2 tsp sugar
1/2 tsp salt
2 medium heads iceberg lettuce
1/2 cup chopped green onions (greens and whites)

In a medium salad bowl, with fork, stir half and half, vinegar, sugar and salt. Mix well. Tear lettuce into bite-sized pieces (do not cut. Add onions to mixture. Toss gently, just enough to coat your iceberg lettuce. (Makes 12 servings.

CLASSIC CREOLE FRENCH DRESSING

3/4 cup olive oil
1/4 cup apple cider or wine vinegar
3/4 tsp salt
Dash pepper

In a small bowl or covered jar, measure all ingredients. Stir with fork or cover and shake until mixed. Cover and refrigerate. Stir or shake before serving. (Makes 1 cup.)

GARLIC: Prepare as above, but add 1 garlic clove. MIXED HERB: Prepare as above, but add 2 tsps chopped parsley, 1/2 tsp tarragon, and 1/2 tsp basil.

RAPHAEL II & EZRA'S QUICK FRENCH DRESSING

1 onion chopped fine
2 cloves garlic, peeled but left whole
1 cup each: oil and vinegar
1 can tomato soup
1 tsp of each: dry mustard, salt, paprika, pepper, and sugar
1 tbsp Worcestershire sauce

Mix and store in a Mason Jar for a few days to improve flavor. Dressing will keep for several weeks.

STELLA MAE HEBERT BOYD'S CREOLE STUFFED PEAR SALAD

1 30 ounce can pear halves
1 8 ounce package cream cheese, softened
2 tbsp mayonnaise
3 tbsp raisins, chopped or whole
1/4 tsp cinnamon
1/2 medium head iceberg lettuce

Drain pear halves, reserving 1/3 cup syrup. In a small bowl, combine half of cream cheese, mayonnaise, and raisins. On waxed paper, drop cream cheese mixture into as many mounds as the number of pear halves for dressing in another bowl. Beat remaining cream cheese, reserved syrup, and cinnamon until creamy. Arrange pear halves on lettuce leaves in round platter. Place a cheese mound in the hollow of each pear half. Serve with dressing and a garnish of grated cheese or carrots.

SOUR CREAM DRESSING

1/2 cup sour cream
1 tbsp lemon juice or apple cider vinegar
3/4 tsp salt

In a cup, stir all ingredients until well mixed. (Makes 1/2 cup.)

THOUSAND ISLAND DRESSING

1 cup mayonnaise
2 tsp chili sauce
4 tbsp minced green pepper (red and yellow optional)
1 tbsp chopped parsley
1 tsp grated onion

In a small bowl, stir all ingredients until well mixed. (Makes about 1 1/3 cups.)

GOOD CREOLE VEGETABLES

The Creole family has carried on a romance with vegetables. Creoles grew them in their gardens, bought them, and stuffed them with a variety of mixtures, like pork, chopped onions and bread crumbs. Many times the Creoles would serve them with a sauce or a hollandaise. They would also mix various vegetables together to compose a symphony of great taste. Oh, we can't forget the Creoles loved to puree, bake, and fry vegetables in a batter too! In this section, we look at the vegetables the Creoles loved so much.

CREOLE SWEET POTATOES
Stella Mae Hebert Boyd

4 to 6 large sweet potatoes
1 stick of butter
2 cups water
1/2 cup sugar
1/4 tsp nutmeg
1/4 cinnamon
1/4 cup Cointreau Orange Liqueur or Grand Marnier (optional)

Peel sweet potatoes. Cut in fourths and place in large pot. Pour 2 cups of water in pot. Add butter, sugar, nutmeg, cinnamon, and Cointreau Orange Liqueur. Boil until sweet potatoes are tender.

TROPICAL CREOLE YAMS (SWEET POTATOES)

Peel and slice yams into 3/4 inch pieces. Grease a casserole dish. Arrange layers of yams, apricot halves, and sliced pineapple. Add raisins and pecan, walnut, or almond chunks over this. Pour juices over all. Top with brown sugar and dot with butter or margarine and marshmallows. Cover and bake at 325° until top is golden brown.

MIRLITON

6 to 12 mirlitons, 6 onions
1 cup salt
1 1/2 quarts white vinegar
6 cups sugar
1/2 cup mustard seeds
1 1/2 tsps celery seeds
2 1/4 tsp cayenne pepper

Soak the mirlitons and onions that have been thinly sliced in a cup of salt with water. Cover in a stone vessel for 3 to 5 hours. Drain and taste. Rinse if too salty. Combine vinegar, sugar, mustard, celery seeds, and pepper. Bring to boil. Simmer for 5 minutes. Add mirliton and onion. Bring just to simmer and hold 3 to 8 minutes or cook longer, then serve or, you can jar and seal hot.

STUFFED EGGPLANT

3 medium eggplants
1 lb. hot pork sausage (bulk)
1 large onion diced
1 clove garlic minced
1/2 cup celery and sweet pepper diced
1 can or 2 tomatoes (about 1 lb.)
1 tsp salt dash black pepper
1/2 cup of each: grated Parmesan cheese and bread crumbs
1/2 tsp sugar

Parboil eggplant in salted water about 10 minutes. Let cool. Brown sausage quickly. Remove all but 2 tbsp fat. Sauté onion, garlic, celery, salt, and green pepper. Add eggplants with tomatoes, sugar, and cheese. Simmer about 5 to 8 minutes more. Top with crumbs mixed with remaining cheese and bake 375° for 45 to 50 minutes.

CREOLE CREAMED CORN

8 ears corn
1 cup cream (heavy optional)
1 cup milk
1 tbsp butter

Put butter, milk, and cream in double boiler and stir constantly until blended. Add raw corn cut from cob, extracting the juices ("milking" well). Mix well. Stir often. Serve hot when corn is cooked. (Takes about 25 minutes).

FRIED OKRA (WHOLE)

1 pound of okra
½ cup of cornmeal
1/2 tsp salt
1/8 tsp pepper

Sprinkle a small amount of cayenne pepper. Remove both ends of okra. Wash well. Cook in boiling salted water for 8 to 10 minutes. Drain and dry. Roll in seasoned cornmeal. Fry in deep fat (hog lard or peanut oil) at 350° or sauté in butter until golden brown.

EMAN MARIE BOYD
CREOLE SCALLOPED POTATOES

2 1/2 lbs. raw potatoes pared and thinly sliced
3 tbsp lour, 4 tbsp butter, and 1 tsp salt
1/8 tsp pepper
2 cups milk

How I Learned to Cook Great Creole Food

Arrange half the slices of potatoes in buttered 1 1/2 quart baking dish. Sprinkle half the flour over potatoes. Place 1 tbsp butter and sprinkle salt and pepper on top of potatoes. Repeat layer of potatoes. For final layer of potatoes, place remaining butter on top. Pour milk over all. Cover and bake in 375° oven 30-40 minutes. Uncover and bake 15 to 18 minutes longer. Garnish with grated cheddar cheese.

EGGPLANT-BACON-GROUND BEEF ROLL UPS

1 medium eggplant, peeled
1/2 pound ground beef
4 tbsp finely chopped celery
1 medium onion, chopped
1 tbsp green pepper, chopped
1 tbsp parsley
2 minced bacon slices
Salt and pepper to taste

Slice eggplant thinly and lengthwise. Place slices in deep dish and salt very well. Let stand for 20 minutes. Rinse in cold water and drain well. Roll each slice around heaping tbsp meat mixture. Wrap in thin slice of bacon, fasten with toothpicks, and place side by side in a baking dish. Cover meat mixture and eggplant with the following mixture: 1 cup water; 1/2 cup tomato paste; 1 small can of mushrooms (or fresh). Bake 1 1/2 to 2 hours uncovered at 350°, turning once during cooking.

CREOLE SNAP BEANS

2 lbs. fresh green beans
3 1/4 lb. ham
4 large onions, chopped
3 cloves garlic, minced
1 1/2 cups water
Salt and pepper

Wash string (snap) beans. Cut into small pieces. Fry ham until light brown. Remove ham. Pour off drippings, except 2 tbsp. Add onions and garlic and cook until onions are soft. Return ham to skillet. Add beans, 1/2 cup water, salt and pepper to taste. Cover, turn heat low, and cook for about 1 1/2 hours. During cooking, occasionally add a little water.

GAYLORD'S STUFFED RAINBOW PEPPERS

6 bell peppers (2 green, 2 red, 2 yellow/gold)
6 tbsp butter
2 onions chopped fine
1 lb. of each: ground pork, ground round, or chuck
4 ribs celery, chopped fine
1/2 tsp garlic powder
1 cup bread crumbs
2 eggs

Salt and pepper to taste Parboil pepper halves and save liquid. Sauté onions and celery in butter. Add cooked pork, round (chuck) and 1/2 cup reserved liquid. Add bread crumbs. Season to taste and add raw eggs. Spoon meat mixture into pepper halves and bake in 350° oven. Cover with 1/2 cup water in pan for 30-40 minutes. Sprinkle tops with remaining bread crumbs.

CREOLE/SEAFOOD STUFFED RAINBOW PEPPERS

Same as recipe before, but use:
1/2 lb. pork
1/2 lb. ground round or chuck
1/4 lb. shrimp (cooked and shredded)
1/4 lb. crawfish tails (cooked and shredded)
1/4 lb. crab meat (cooked and shredded)

CORA G. HEBERT'S (ME' MA'S)
HASH BROWNED POTATOES

3 cups cubed cooked potatoes
1 tbsp bacon fat
1/4 cup milk
1 tbsp minced parsley
1 small onion
2 tbsp butter
Salt and pepper

Heat bacon fat in skillet at 365°. Combine remaining ingredients, except butter, place in skillet and pack into large cake pan. Dot with butter, lower your heat to 340°, and cover for about 2 minutes. When butter is melted, remove cover. Cook about 6 to 8 minutes or until brown on bottom. Turn and brown the other side about 6 to 8 minutes. (Serves 4 to 6.)

FELIX HEBERT, SR.
PA PA'S AU GRATIN POTATOES

2 tbsp of each: butter and all-purpose flour
1 tsp salt
1 1/2 cups milk
1/4 lb. sharp cheddar cheese
1/4 cup bread crumbs
1 -1/2 lbs. boiled potatoes, sliced

Preheat oven to 350°. Butter 1 ½ quart casserole dish. Melt butter. Blend in flour and salt. Stir until smooth. Turn heat to low and slowly add milk, stirring. Cook and stir until thick and smooth. Remove from heat. Add cheese, stir until it melts. Arrange potatoes in buttered 1 1/2 quart casserole. Pour cheese sauce over potatoes, and top with bread crumbs. Dot with butter. Bake in 350° oven 17 to 22 minutes or until brown (Serves 4.)

CREOLE BLACK EYE PEAS

3 quarts water
1 lb black-eyed peas
1 large onion, diced
3 cloves garlic, chopped
5 bay leaves
1 bell pepper, diced
½ Tbsp liquid smoke
1 link sliced andouille sausage
1 tbsp lard of back fat
Salt and pepper

Wash and rinse peas well. Add water, onion garlic, bell pepper, and lard or bacon fat. Cover and cook for 1 to 1 1/2 hours on medium heat. Add andouille and bay leaves. Cook covered until creamy (about 2 or 2 1/2 hours. Salt and pepper to taste. (Serves 8.)

CREOLE RED BEANS (SAME RECIPE AS ABOVE, BUT USE RED BEANS)

STUFFED CREOLE TOMATOES

6 large tomatoes
1/4 lb. minced ham
2 medium onions, minced
4 sprigs parsley, minced fine
3 cloves garlic, minced
1 can of tomatoes
1 1/4 tbsp butter
Bread crumbs, toasted
Salt and pepper to taste

Cut tomatoes in half horizontally and scoop out pulp and seeds. Salt and place hollowed insides upside down on a sheet pan lined with parchment paper. Place pulp and seeds into pot. Add tomatoes and cook down (stew). Fry ham, onions, and butter in skillet. Add ham mixture to pot. Add parsley and garlic to pot. Add salt and pepper to taste. Cook until reduced but not dry. Remove from stove. Fill hollowed tomato halves with ham mix-ture and bake until light brown. Place bread crumbs on top of stuffed tomatoes before baking. (Makes 12 halves.)

CHINESE/CREOLE FRIED RICE

2 eggs (beaten)
4 tbsp peanut oil
1/4 cup green onions, cut in 1/4 inch circular pieces
1/2 cup chopped carrots
2 tbsp soy sauce

1/2 tsp light brown sugar
1/2 cup sweet peas
1 cup shrimp (cooked)
1 small green pepper chopped/diced
4 cups cold cooked rice
2-3 sprigs minced parsley
Scramble eggs slightly. (Do not add milk or water.)

Set aside 1 tbsp oil. Heat remaining peanut oil over high heat. Add green onions, carrots, peas, peppers and stir. Add rice and stir quickly so rice won't stick. Make sure rice is well coated with peanut oil. Add soy sauce and sugar. Mix well and add shrimp and eggs, mixing and breaking eggs in small pieces. (Serves 4-6.)

BREADS Bread, Bread - Let's Bake Creole Style

CREOLE "SCRATCH" BISCUITS

1/4 cup shortening
2 cups sifted all purpose flour
1 tsp salt
4 tsps baking powder
3/4 to 1 cup milk

Blend shortening into sifted dry ingredients. Add milk slowly to form soft dough. Knead 1/2 to 1 minute on lightly floured board. Roll out to 1/2 inch thickness. Cut with biscuit cutter (floured). Place on greased cookie sheet. Bake at 450° for 13 to 17 minutes. (Yields 12.)

CREOLE CORN BREAD

1 tsp soda
2 tsps salt
1/4 tsp baking powder
1 cups cornmeal (yellow or white)

1/4 cup sugar
3 tbsp shortening
1/2 cup flour
2 cups buttermilk

Put sugar, salt, baking soda, and baking powder in a bowl. Add buttermilk. Stir well. Add cornmeal and flour alternately. Melt shortening in loaf pan and add to mixture. Sprinkle a little cornmeal in loaf pan. Heat pan. Pour mixture into hot pan. Bake at 350° in oven for 47 to 63 minutes. (Yields 16-18 squares.)

HUSH PUPPIES

1/2 cup flour (sifted)
1 cup cornmeal
1 onion, minced
1 1/2 tsp baking powder
1 egg
1 tsp salt
1 tsp sugar
1/2 cup half and half (or light cream or milk)
(2 small jalapeno peppers, minced if desired)

Combine all ingredients. Drop from spoon in hot oil (350°) and cook 3-5 minutes until golden brown. (Makes 24 hush puppies.)

CINNAMON COFFEE CAKE

Juice of 1 lemon
1 cup powdered Sugar
¼ cup chopped pecans and walnuts
¼ cup sugar
1 tsp Cinnamon
1 package white cake mix
½ pint sour cream
4 eggs
¾ cup salad oil
2 tsps rum

Blend cake mix, ½ cup sugar, sour cream, oil, and eggs to form batter. Set aside. Mix cinnamon, ¼ cup sugar and pecans. Place ¼ of mixture on bottom of a tube pan. Add ½ cake batter.

Sprinkle ¼ nut mixture on top of cake batter. Then pour in the rest of the batter. Top with remaining nut mixture and bake at 325° degrees for 1 hour and 10 minutes. Glaze while warm with a mixture of powdered sugar, lemon juice, and 2 tsps of rum

(FELIX HEBERT JR'S)
Lost Creole Bread

2 tbsp sugar
1/4 cup Half and Half
1/8 tsp salt
1/4 tsp brandy and vanilla
2 eggs beaten
6 slices of bread (wheat, white, Roman Meal, etc.)
2 tbsp shortening
1 to 1 1/2 tbsp butter or bacon droppings
Confection sugar
Honey and sugar (use best judgment)

Combine sugar, Half and Half, salt, flavoring, brandy, and eggs. Soak bread in mixture, cook in hot shortening and butter until well browned on both sides. Sprinkle with confection sugar. Drape with honey and syrup. (Makes 8 servings.)

CREOLE CINNAMON ROLLS

5 lbs all purpose flour
1 quart milk (reserve ¼ cup)
2 cups sugar   3 packages yeast
¼ cup warm water
1 tsp salt
2 tsps baking powder
1 tsp baking soda
1 cup vegetable shortening or peanut oil
8 quart pot

With floured rolling pin, roll dough out to a 10" x 13" rectangle 1 inch thick. Mix cinnamon and sugar together. Spread evenly over dough and seal edges. Cut into 1 inch rings. Place on cookie sheet and let rise for 1 hour. Bake at 375° until brown.

ROLL TOPPING

2 cups powdered sugar
½ cup brown sugar
1 tbsp butter   ¼ cup milk

Warm milk in saucepan. DO NOT BOIL! Add butter. Once butter has melted remove saucepan from fire. Sift powdered sugar with brown sugar and place in bowl. Add milk mixture, a few drops at a time to sifted sugar to make topping easy to spread or drop on top of each roll.

ISLAND COUSH-COUSH (VENTRESS, LA)

2 tsps shortening
3 eggs beaten
2 tsps baking powder
2 cups corn meal
½ tsp salt
1-1/2 cup boiling water

Stir corn meal and salt into boiling water. Cool and add baking powder and eggs. Preheat skillet with shortening and pour in mixture. Cook over medium heat 5 to 7 minutes. (Makes 8 servings.)

CORIENE JACKSON
"NAN CORIENE" CREOLE/NEW ORLEANS BEIGNETS

Oil for deep frying
1 package yeast
1 tsp salt
1 fresh egg (brown is best)
1 tsp nutmeg
1 cup milk scalded
1 tbsp brown sugar
2 tbsp butter, margarine, or vegetable shortening
1 tbsp sugar
3 cups enriched plain flour, sifted

Heat milk in sauce pan to scalding stage. DO NOT SCORCH. Stir often. Place shortening in a mixing bowl and add sugar. Pour in scalded milk and stir until ingredients are melted. Cool to lukewarm stage. Add yeast, stir until yeast is dissolved. Sift dry ingredients - salt, nutmeg and flour. Slowly add approximately 1/2 of flour mixture to milk mixture to form your batter. Add whole egg. Beat thoroughly. Stir in remaining flour mixture. Cover. Set aside to allow batter to double in bulk (about 1 hour). Knead gently. Rollout on floured board to 1 inch thickness. Cut in diamond shapes. Cover. Let rise in warm place from 1 to 1 1/2 hour. Fry in hot oil at 385°, turning only once. Drain and dust with confectioners' sugar. Serve warm.

CREOLE BAR-B-QUE THE OLD-FASHIONED WAY!

The Creole culture used cooking outdoors as another form of family togetherness, at wed-dings, birthdays, reunions and other events too numerous to mention. They knew direction, as well as recipes, for cooking outdoors must be more general than for food preparation in the kitchen. Much depends on the amount of heat from the grill or open fires, as well as the current air temperature and even the amount of wind. The Creole cook, however, always selected simple-easy-to-cook foods. He or she knew that many great meals in the open were always the best tasting. Ahead are a few of the family's great bar-b-que recipes. So, get ready to cook in the great outdoors. Here is a list of favorites to bar-b-que Creole style: chicken, spare ribs (beef or pork, fish, shrimp, lobster, crawfish, rock Cornish hens, ham, pork steaks, sirloins, New York strips, T-bones (or Porter House steaks, ribeye steaks, chuck steak, hamburgers, hot dogs, smoke sausage, skewered sausages, corn on the cob with shuck, vegetables, rib steaks, lamb, and turkey.

EQUIPMENT

A grill of your choice, heavy-duty foil, charcoal starter or lighter fluid (no gas or alcohol, tongs, baster brush, fork, special racks for shrimp and fish, grill thermometer, drip pans, sauces, water, and liquid smoke.

GRILLING TECHNIQUES

Direct heat: Arrange the coals so the food can be worked directly over it (grill open or cover for direct heat.

Indirect heat: Arrange drip pan (heavy-duty in center of grill. Arrange coals around drip pan. To gauge the temperature. Use a grill thermometer or hold your hand, palm down, above the coals and count in long seconds, 1 thousand 1, etc. If you can keep your hand over the coals for no more than 2 seconds, the coals are hot (about 400°) 3 to 4 seconds medium heat (about 350°), 5 to 6 seconds low heat (300°).

CREOLE BAR-B-QUE SEASONING RUB

Salt
1 1/2 tbsp Accent
2 tbsp sugar (brown)
3 tbsp black pepper
1 tbsp cayenne pepper
1/2 tbsp onion powder
1 tbsp chili powder
1 tbsp paprika
1 tbsp garlic powder
(Use the amounts you want to make as much as you need.)

CREOLE GLAZES for (HAMS or RACK OF LAMB)

Grape jelly, honey brown sugar, grey poupon or Creole mustard

CREOLE BAR-B-QUE MUSTARD SAUCE for (RIBS)

Mix garlic, brown sugar, Creole mustard, horse radish, and yellow mustard, and brush with honey at end of cooking.

VENTRESS ISLAND SAUCE for (PORK LOINS or CHOPS)

Reduced pork stock Creole, brown and yellow mustard, horse radish, catsup, onion, green onion, garlic, brown sugar. Sauté vegetables. Then add to mixture.

SHRIMP KABABS

1 lb cleaned, peeled shrimp (leave tails on)
Bacon
Cherry tomatoes
Mushroom
Pineapple chunks
12 wooden kabab skewers
Onion, chopped in chunks
Bell pepper, chopped in chunks
Kabab sauce (BBQ sauce, honey, and Creole custard)

Soak wooden kabab skewers for 15 minutes. Light grill. Thread shrimp and vegetables on each skewer, leaving about an inch from top to bottom of the skewer. Repeat threading on each kabab skewer. Brush skewers with kabab sauce before placing on grill. Turn skewers once. Remove when shrimp have turned pink.

BAR-B-QUE BAKED BEANS

2 pounds of beans or a 12 ounce can baked beans
1/3 cup sherry
3 tbsp brown sugar
1 tsp instant coffee powder
1 tsp dry mustard
1 tbsp lemon juice
2 3/4 cup ketchup
3 large onions mixed
1/2 tsp liquid smoke

Combine all ingredients. Place mixture in casserole and bake in 300° oven about 1 1/2 to 2 hours. (Serves 4.)

GAYLORD'S BAKED BEANS

1 can pork and beans
I small box (individual serving) raisins
1 small Granny Smith apple (diced into small pieces)
4 strips lean bacon
4-6 tbsp bar-b-que sauce
1/2 Tbsp brown sugar
1/2 cup chopped onions

CREOLE ONION RINGS

1 1/2 cups all-purpose lour
4 heaping tbsp corn meal
3 heaping tsps onion powder
2 tsps salt
1/2 cup Half and Half, heavy cream, or milk
1 large egg
1/2 cup water

Mix all ingredients well. Coat 1 to 1 1/2 inch onion ring slices with mixture. Deep fry at 375° until golden, not brown.

CREOLE CHICKEN WINGS/RIB SAUCE

4 tbsp of each sesame seeds, peanut butter, brown sugar
2 tsps curry powder
1/2 cup soy sauce
1/3 cup peanut oil
3 Green onions (white only)
2 tbsp minced garlic
Dash grated ginger root
1/3 cup cherry wine

Place all ingredients in blender and blend to liquid. Rub chicken wings or ribs with spices from blender. Chill for 2 to 3 hours and grill.

CREOLE ROAST RUB (GRILL OR OVEN)
Boneless pork roast, chuck roast, rump roast

1 tbsp liquid smoke
3-4 cloves garlic, chopped or minced
1 cup onions, finely chopped
2 tbsp Worcestershire sauce
2 tbsp teak sauce
2 tbsp mustard (your choice, Creole or yellow)

Blend ingredients together in blender. Cut large slits in meat and fill with blended mixture. Grill or oven roast.

CREOLE BAR-B-QUE SAUCE

1 1/2 cups ketchup
3 tbsp cider vinegar
2 tbsp dark com syrup or cane syrup
2 tsps salt
1 tsp paprika
3/4 tsp chili powder
1/4 cup steak sauce (your choice)

In a medium bowl, combine all ingredients. Use to baste spare ribs, beef, or lamb during grilling.

CREOLE POTATO SALAD

5 medium potatoes
½ cup finely chopped celery
½ cup sliced green onion
¼ tsp salt
1/8 tsp pepper
¼ tsp sweet pickle relish
2 hard boiled eggs, chopped (reserve yellow)
1 1/2 tbsp yellow mustard (or Creole or brown mustard)
2 parsley sprigs inely chopped
3 tbsp mayonnaise
Dash of paprika

In a pot, cook potatoes in boiling, salted water with peel (skin on for 24 to 35 minutes or until tender. Drain, peel, and slice potatoes. Combine celery, green onion, relish, salt, pepper, egg whites, mustard, parsley, and mayonnaise. Add potatoes to mixture until well blended. Garnish with celery sprig, parsley sprigs, and dust with paprika.

CREOLE CORN ON THE COB

4 to 12 ears of corn
1/2 tsp ground cumin
1/2 tsp ground red pepper
1 stick unsalted butter
1/2 tsp garlic powder
1 tbsp lime juice
Lemon
Pepper seasoning

Heat grill. Mix juice and seasonings, except lemon pepper. Pull corn shucks back and remove silk. Clean cobs well. Add seasoning to cobs and rub with butter. Sprinkle lemon pepper on corn. Close shucks. Place on grill 20 to 35 minutes until tender, turning 1/4 turn every 7 minutes.

CREOLE COLESLAW

4 cups finely shredded cabbage (2 cups red, 2 cups green)
1 cup celery (thinly sliced)
1/2 cup mayonnaise
2 large carrots (thinly sliced)
2 tbsp vinegar
1/2 cup milk
1 tsp prepared mustard
1/2 tsp sugar
1 tbsp chopped pimiento
1/4 tsp salt
1/4 tsp paprika

Combine cabbage, celery, carrots, and green pepper. Stir together mayonnaise, vinegar, mustard, sugar, salt, paprika and milk. Pour mixture over vegetables, toss to coat vegetables. Cover and chill. Garnish with pimiento.

GUMBO! GUMBO! GUMBO!

Creole gumbo has deep roots in the Creole culture. From the communal pot of okra simmering on a fire in an African village, gumbo is something like magic when it's all put together. Most of all, it taste good. Always classified as a one-dish meal, nourishing and filling, gumbo will stay with you. Gumbo is like a snowflake… Well, not exactly, but the same principles apply. There are many ways to make gumbo, and no two gumbos are alike. Even experienced cooks cannot make it exactly the same way twice. Traditional Creole cooks could take chicken or turkey, a piece of sausage, some shrimp, crabs, a little of this and a little of that, and make a great gumbo. As I mentioned earlier, there are many types of gumbo. You have seafood gumbo, chicken gumbo, turkey gumbo, duck gumbo, sausage gumbo, and okra and filé gumbo. Regardless of what type you decide to make, two rules always apply: You start off with a roux, and you'll either use okra or filé as a thickening and flavoring element. Making the gumbo requires several utensils: a big iron black skillet, a big pot, and smaller pots for steaming. Careful preparation of ingredients to be placed in your gumbo is also important.

THE ROUX

Melt butter in a skillet or use cooking oil. Add flour and stir over even heat until dark brown. (Keep the fire very low.) Once this is done, add chopped onions, scallions, and garlic and stir them in well. Cook vegetables until they are transparent. Remember, be careful not to burn your vegetables. Now, you're ready to make your choice of gumbos.

SO, ON WITH THE GUMBO VARIETIES

CREOLE SEAFOOD GUMBO

3 dozen large crabs, crab claws, or crabmeat
3 lb. fresh, medium to large shrimp
2 large onions, chopped
1/4 cup fresh chopped parsley

3 cloves minced garlic
crab and shrimp boil
1 medium pack of dried shrimp
1 to 2 dozen oysters
Green onions (shallots), chopped

Peel the shrimp. Do not de-vein. Save heads and shells. Wash and clean crabs thoroughly (if they are live). Place in a large pot, then cover with boiling water and a dash of salt. Cook crabs for 15 to 25 minutes. Take them out of the pot and place them in the sink to cool. Save stock. Crush shrimp shells and heads. Add this mixture to crab stock, along with mixture of oyster liquid in stock pot. These ingredients make a great rich stock for gumbo. Boil for 30 minutes. With your basic Creole roux already prepared, in a heavy skillet, sauté vegetables until transparent. Strain your stock (with shrimp heads and shells). Add vegetables and oysters on a low fire. Simmer for 25 minutes. Add crabs (make sure crabs are broken into pieces that is claws, legs, body cavity, etc.). Add remaining ingredients and simmer for about 1 hour (do not let mixture boil, just cover on low heat to simmer). Serve over rice with a little filé'. (Serves 8 to 12.)

CREOLE SHRIMP, TASSO, SAUSAGE, AND OKRA GUMBO

The cousins to Creoles, the Cajuns, have a type of dried beef called tasso. It's like the beef jerky of the Western cowboys or frontiersmen. Rubbed with salt and various spices, it is great, especially when combined with shrimp, sausage, and okra.

2 lbs. tasso
3 lbs. fresh shrimp
3 lbs. fresh or frozen okra chopped
3 lbs. onions, chopped
4 cloves garlic, minced
4 tbsp bacon drippings
1/4 tsp cayenne pepper

Cover the tasso chunks with water and soak overnight. Drain or save tasso in water or cover with fresh water and boil gently for 1 1/2 to 2 hours. Cover shrimp with the water the tasso was boiled in and boil for 5 minutes. Remove shrimp, peel, and set aside. This stock may be too strong and salty. Taste. If too strong or salty, dilute with fresh water. Add your prepared roux and okra, and cook until the okra loses its gummy or slimy consistency. Add cayenne pepper and stir well. Place mixture in large pot and add tasso-shrimp stock to cover about 1 to 1 1/2 inches. If necessary, add water. Cook at a slow simmer for 45 to 55 minutes. Add salt and black pepper if necessary. Serve in a gumbo bowl with a little rice. Add filé or let your guests do it to their tastes.

SEAFOOD, SAUSAGE, CHICKEN & FILÉ GUMBO

2 lbs. large boiled shrimp (save water and shells)
1 chicken or hen, cut up (about 3 lb.)
1/4 cup chopped parsley
1 lb. andouille sausage cut in small circles
1/2 lb. smoked sausage
2 large onions chopped
4 green onions (scallions chopped ine)
2 tbsp filé powder
6 large crabs (cleaned, broken into pieces)
1 small or medium pack of dried shrimp

Place cut-up chicken or hen in skillet with butter or oil and cook (do not brown). Boil andouille and smoked sausages in pot for about 35 to 45 minutes. Remove chicken and sausage. Save broth from sausage. Remove chicken or hen meat from the bone. In a large pot, to your prepared roux mixture, add the chicken, sausage, andouille, and liquid from the chicken and sausage. Add water or a chicken bouillon cube if needed. Simmer for about 1 hour. Add shrimp (boiled), green onions, parsley, and simmer for 5 to 11 minutes. Add 2 tbsp of filé powder (or place filé on the table and let your guests add their own. Serve in a gumbo bowl with a little rice.

ON WITH SEAFOOD!

FRIED SHRIMP WITH SESAME SEEDS

Peeled raw de-veined shrimp, medium to large
Sesame seeds
1 cup beer (your choice)
Peanut oil
1/2 tsp baking powder
1 cup flour, sifted
1/8 tsp black or red pepper
1 tsp salt

In a mixing bowl, place 1 cup beer, sifted flour, baking powder and pepper. Mix well. Add more beer if needed. (Works best when you let it set for 2-3 hours, but you can use it immediately). Make sure shrimp is dry after washing. Use deep skillet or deep fryer. Put in peanut oil. Heat to 370 to 378°. Dip shrimp in batter and then dip in sesame seeds. Place shrimp in skillet or deep fryer (use wine basket). Fry quickly until golden (but not brown).

CREOLE TARTAR SAUCE

1 cup premium mayonnaise (your choice)
2 tbsp finely chopped onion
2 tbsp chopped sweet pickle
1 tbsp finely chopped parsley
Juice from 1 lemon

Mix all ingredients well and chill before using.

CREOLE MUSTARD AND HONEY SHRIMP

Salt to taste
Juice of 1 lemon
1 cup honey
1/2 stick butter
2 1/2 to 3 lbs. peeled shrimp
1/2 cup Creole mustard

Melt 1/2 stick butter in skillet and cook shrimp 1 1/2 minutes until pink. Add lemon juice, honey, Creole mustard, and salt. Simmer for 2 to 3 minutes longer. Serve with noodles or the pasta of your choice.

BUTTERFLY FRIED SHRIMP

(Use beer in sesame seed shrimp recipe.)

2 lbs. raw shrimp in the shells Peel the shrimp, leaving in the last segment of the shell and the tail on. Hold each shrimp on its back. Split it down the inside with a small sharp knife, cutting the tail toward the front. Do not cut all the way through until the final inch or half inch. Spread the shrimp out in the butterfly shape. Dry well with paper towels. Hold each shrimp by the tail and dip in beer batter. Place shrimp in bottom of frying basket. Cooking time is 1 to 1 1/2 minutes, until golden, not brown. Serve with tartar sauce, soy sauce, or bar-b-que sauce.

RAINBOW CREOLE SHRIMP STUFFED GREEN PEPPERS

1 1/2 lbs. cooked, peeled shrimp
1 medium onion chopped
2 tbsp minced celery
2 tbsp chopped fresh parsley
1 tsp Worcestershire sauce
1/2 cup tomato sauce
2 cups cooked brown and wild rice (more depending on size of your peppers)
2 tbsp butter
1/2 cup bread crumbs (plain or seasoned)
12 peppers (green, yellow, and red)
1/4 tsp cayenne pepper
2 tbsp white wine
Salt and black pepper

Cut the shrimp into 1/4" pieces. Save 12 whole shrimp to garnish the tops of peppers. Cook onions and celery in butter until tender. Add parsley, Worcestershire, cayenne, salt, black pepper, and tomato sauce. Cook for about 5 minutes. Add cooked rice and mix thoroughly. Cut tops of peppers to form cups. Remove seeds and inside pulp. Cover with hot water. Add salt and par boil for 5 to 15 minutes, until soft. Rinse in cold water to stop cooking process. Drain well. Fill peppers with the shrimp-rice mixture. Add a little bread crumbs to thicken. Top each pepper after stuffing with more bread crumbs. Place peppers in greased casserole. Add 1/4" water. Bake for 20 to 35 minutes at 375°. Garnish with finely chopped parsley and whole shrimp (reserved) on top.

CREOLE SEAFOOD JAMBALAYA

2 lbs. raw shrimp, peeled
2 cups raw brown rice
1 lb andouille sausage
½ lb Creole smoked sausage
1/2 lb. crab meat
1/2 lb. cooked chicken (white meat diced)
1/2 stick butter
4 tbsp flour
2 16 oz cans beef broth
4 cloves garlic, minced
2 medium onions, chopped ine
6 green onions chopped (including green part)
1 small green pepper chopped
1 bay leaf
½ tsp thyme
1/8 tsp cumin
1/8 tsp ground allspice
1/4 to 1/2 tsp cayenne
Salt and black pepper

Melt butter in black pot or Dutch oven. Cook sausage and andouille until lightly brown and stir in flour. Add onions, green onions, green pepper ,and garlic. Cook until soft and transparent. Stir in bay leaf, thyme, cumin, all spice, cayenne, salt and black pepper. Add broth and mix well. Add raw shrimp, crab, and chicken. Stir in raw rice. Liquid should cover contents. Add more broth if needed. Bring to boil. Drop to low heat. Cover the pot and simmer until rice is done. Remember, jambalaya should be moist but not soupy.

CRABS, CRABS, CREOLE CRABS!

The favorite way the Creoles loved to cook crabs was to boil them. This incredible crustacean is one of the greatest gifts to Louisiana and other states bordering the Gulf of Mexico. Aside from the gulf, they can be found in bayous, swamps, and streams. To the Creoles, eating boiled crabs was almost a ritual. They knew that boiling them was about as much fun as eating them. This section is dedicated to the incredible crab.

CREOLE BOILED CRABS

48 live crabs (4 dozen)
4 3-5 oz. packages crab boil (choose our brand)
4 large onions (chopped or halves)
2 to 3 lemons, sliced
5 tbsp cayenne pepper
1/2 lb. salt and accent
1 1/2 bunches parsley
7 ribs celery with leaves, chopped
6 large potatoes cut in half (new potatoes or Idaho)
10 ears of corn

Estimate how much water it will take to cover the crabs. After washing and cleaning them, place them in a large pot. Boil all ingredients for 1/2 hour to make a good rich liquor. Make sure the crabs are all live and kicking around. At this point, add enough hot water to completely cover them. When water comes to a boil, cook for 25 to 35 minutes. Take the crabs out and let them cool. If you cook more crabs, use the same pot and ingredients over and over. The stronger, the better. If you don't know how to eat them, ask a Creole to help you.

LUMP CRABMEAT AND CREOLE CRAWFISH

1/4 cup tomato sauce
1/2 cup dry white wine
½ stick butter
3 finely chopped green onions
1 sprig parsley, finely chopped
1/4 tsp chopped garlic
1 lb. cooked and peeled crawfish tails
1/2 lb. lump crabmeat
1/4 cup crawfish fat (from shells of boiled crawfish)

From our section on gumbo, make a light roux, about 1 1/2 cups.
Melt the butter and cook onions, parsley, and garlic until soft. Add wine and tomato sauce and cook for about 3 to 6 minutes. Add the sauce (roux) and bring to a light simmer. Add crabmeat, crawfish, and fat (season with Creole seasoning recipe in front section of book), salt, and pepper, and return to simmer. Serve hot in small dishes.

STUFFED CREOLE CRABS AU GRATIN

2 lbs. crabmeat
12 crab shells
1/4 cup grated cheddar cheese (mild)
1/2 cup grated Swiss cheese
1 cup chopped fresh mushrooms
1/2 tsp powdered mustard
1/3 stick butter
2 tbsp flour
1 cup heavy cream
1 cup Half and Half
Salt and pepper
A pinch of nutmeg

Preheat oven to 400°. Melt butter in a skillet. Add flour and mix well. Remove from heat and add Half and Half slowly, stirring constantly. Add cream the same way. Return to fire and add grated cheeses. Cook until a smooth mixture develops. Add mushrooms, mustard, nutmeg, salt, and pepper and stir. After the sauce thickens, fill the bottom of each crab shell with sauce. Then fill each shell with crabmeat. Repeat the process, filling the bottom of each crab shell with sauce and then crabmeat.. Bake in the oven for 1 hour.

CRAB MEAT RAPHAEL and EZRA JOSEPH

1 lb. crabmeat
1 small head lettuce
1 cup mayonnaise
1/2 cup tomato sauce (fresh, if not canned)
Juice of 1/4 lemon
Juice of 1/4 lime
1 tbsp capers
1/4 tsp cayenne pepper
Salt and coarse black pepper

Remove the coarse lettuce leaves. Shred the leaves. Mix in mayonnaise, tomato sauce, lemon and lime juice, capers, cayenne, salt, and pepper. Add lettuce to the mixture. Add crabmeat and mix. Stir but do not break up crabmeat. Serve in four individual salad bowls.

EAT OYSTERS; LIVE LONGER

The Creole cuisine has many, and I mean many, good ways to cook oysters. Oysters are magic. Oysters are a miracle. Wholesome results are obtained because they contain zinc and magnesium. Enough of that, you can read about oysters in another book. On with the recipes.

CREOLE FRIED OYSTERS

To get the best results, when frying oysters, use yellow corn flour. The Creoles never used cornmeal because it's too coarse and will not cook thoroughly. No batter is needed to fry oysters. The oil to use is peanut oil and the best fat is hog lard. Always deep fry. Pre-heat oil or fat. Season flour with salt and pepper. Select your oysters. Roll lightly in seasoned flour. Fry in hot oil or fat about 250-260° for 2 to 3 1/2 minutes. When done, they will be a light golden brown. Serve with lemon wedges, tartar sauce, or oyster cocktail sauce. Use a little dash of Tabasco. The Creoles never used ketchup on nice, tasty oysters.

OYSTER COCKTAIL SAUCE

2 tbsp horseradish
1 tbsp fresh lemon juice
1/2 tbsp fresh lime juice
1/2 tsp Tabasco

1 bottle tomato chili sauce
Salt and pepper
1/2 tsp garlic juice
1/2 tsp onion juice

Mix all ingredients well and chill. Place in small container or spread on top of oyster, and get ready to enjoy.

CREOLE OYSTER PO BOY LOAF

2 dozen fried oysters
1 16 to 20" loaf of bread, with butter
Lettuce, pickles, and tomato slices
Mayonnaise, and oyster cocktail sauce

Split the loaf of bread about 1/2 in down, toast lightly, and brush with butter. Pile oysters on toasted slices and cover with lettuce, tomato, pickle, and mayonnaise and/or cocktail sauce. Cut in half, they are ready to serve 1 or 2.

CREOLE BACON-WRAPPED OYSTERS

1 dozen oysters
6 slices thick bacon

Cut bacon slices in half. Fry in skillet until limp. Wrap each bacon piece around an oyster. Skewer with toothpicks. Place wrapped oysters in broiler pan. Broil until bacon is brown and oyster edges are curled.

OH BOY, CRAWFISH!

The little town of Breaux Bridge is known throughout the state as the Crawfish Capital of the World. Located on Bayou Teche, Breaux Bridge or Palm Breaux produces about 27 mil-lion pounds of crawfish a year. Breaux Bridge celebrates its Crawfish Festival in the spring of each year, and many Creoles come from surrounding cities and towns to experience what the Cajuns called "mud bugs," those self-reproducing, easy to capture, and good to eat creatures. After they are caught, the joy of feasting begins. I've covered just a few ways the Creoles cooked these "mud bugs," crawfish, or crawdads. I hope you enjoy them!

CREOLE WAY TO BOIL CRAWFISH

(Added way to boil adapted from the Cajuns)

1 50 lb. sack of crawfish, live
12 peeled onions, cut in half
1 bunch celery with leaves, chopped
2 bunches parsley, chopped
4 to 5 heads unpeeled garlic
7 3oz. packages of crab or shrimp boil
3 to 5 oz. cayenne
12 ears corn
12 red new potatoes, unpeeled

Use a 30 gallon garbage can or large pot. Fill it with water. Add all ingredients, except the crawfish. Bring to a boil for 30 to 35 minutes, until it begins to roll. Clean the crawfish well in salted water and discard all the dead ones. When cleaned, add them to the boiling water. Add potatoes and corn and wait until the water is back to a rolling boil. Add the crawfish and cook for 15 to 17 minutes. Turn off heat. Test one crawfish. If not spicy enough, allow them to soak in the mixture for a few more minutes or adjust the seasoning by adding more cayenne.

CREOLE CRAWFISH ETOUFFE (SMOTHERED)

2 lb. crawfish tails, boiled, cleaned and de-veined
1/2 cup crawfish fat
1 large onion, finely chopped
2 green onions, with leaves chopped
2 ribs celery, finely chopped
1 small green bell pepper, chopped
2 cloves minced garlic
1 stick butter
1/2 tbsp flour
2 cups water
Salt and pepper
A dash of cayenne pepper

Melt the butter in a black iron skillet. Add flour and cook on low heat, stirring to make a peanut-butter-colored roux. Add onions, green onions, celery, green pepper, and garlic. Cook until limp. Add crawfish fat and water. Season with salt, pepper, and cayenne. Simmer for 15 minutes. Add crawfish. Simmer for 10 more minutes. Let set 1/2 hour before serving. Serve on a plate or bowl over hot steamed rice (or you can use wild rice with mushrooms). Garnish with the green part of your green onions.

CREOLE FRIED CRAWFISH

2 lb. crawfish tails cleaned and de-veined
3 eggs
1/4 cup Half and Half or heavy cream
Flour
Salt and pepper
Cayenne pepper

Season cleaned tails with pepper, salt, and cayenne pepper. Season flour. Beat eggs. Add Half and Half until the right consistency exists. Dip each crawfish tail into the mixture and deep fry in hog lard or peanut oil until lightly golden.

CREOLE SWEET TREATS

CORA HEBERT FIGARO
NINA'S CREOLE BAKED BANANAS

4 firm ripe bananas
1 tsp cinnamon
2 tbsp sugar
1 tsp nutmeg
1/2 cup honey
8 tbsp butter

Peel and clean bananas, cut them in half, and then cut each half lengthwise. Arrange the pieces in a casserole dish and sprinkle them with cinnamon, sugar, and nutmeg. Pour honey generously over the top, dot with small pieces of butter, and bake in the oven at 300-325° for 20 to 25 minutes. (Serves about 6.)

APPLE CRISP CREOLE

8 apples sliced
1/2 cup butter
3/4 cup sugar
1/2 cup water
1 tsp cinnamon
1/2 cup flour

Peel and slice apples very thin. Fill casserole dish with apple slices, water, and cinnamon. Blend remaining ingredients until crumbly in texture. Spread mixture over top of apples and bake uncovered in hot 425° oven for 50 to 60 minutes. (Serves 6-8.)

PECAN PIE

1/2 tbsp granulated sugar
1/2 tbsp brown sugar
1/2 tsp vanilla
1/2 pint whipping cream
1 prepared pie shell
1 pint praline pecan ice cream
1/2 cup chopped pecans

Bake pie shell in 350° oven for 12 to 17 minutes. Cool, fill with softened ice cream, and freeze. Top with the whipping cream that contains the vanilla and sugars. Place it back in freezer until just before you are ready to serve.

CREOLE BREAD PUDDING

1 loaf stale French bread
1 cup raisins
3 tbsp butter
2 tbsp vanilla
1 quart milk
3 eggs
1 cup sugar and brown sugar

Soak stale bread in milk. Crush with hands until well mixed. Add eggs, sugar, vanilla, and raisins. Stir well. Pour melted butter in bottom of thick pan and bake until very firm. Let cool. Cube pudding and put it in individual dessert dishes. When ready to serve, add the whiskey sauce, and heat under broiler.

CREOLE WHISKEY SAUCE

Whiskey to taste
1 cup sugar
8 tbsp butter

Cream butter and sugar. Cook in a double boiler until very hot and sugar is well dissolved. Add well-beaten egg and whip fast so egg doesn't curdle or scramble. Let cool and add whiskey.

ENAISE JACKSON'S CREOLE COCONUT CAKE

1 tsp vanilla
1 cup milk
4 eggs
1 cup sugar
8 tbsp butter
¼ tsp salt
4 tsps baking powder
2 cups flour, sifted

Mix baking powder and salt with sifted flour. Cream butter and add sugar slowly, continuing to cream while you add. Beat eggs, and do not separate yolks and whites. Add your creamed butter/sugar mixture to sifted flour mixture. Slowly alternate with your milk. Add vanilla flavoring and beat to mix well. Pour into well-greased or buttered pans and bake. (Makes 2 9" layers, 3 8" layers, or 25 cupcakes.) **Layer temperatures:** 375° for 31 to 36 minutes. **Cupcake temperatures:** 375° for 17 to 22 minutes.

FILLING FOR CAKE OR TO TOP MUFFINS/CUP CAKES

1/4 cup sugar
1/4 cup brown sugar
1/4 cup flour
1/2 cup water

1 tbsp corn starch
½ cup coconut milk
1 tbsp butter
Shredded coconut

In a double boiler, mix sugars, flour, water, and corn starch. Cook mixture until it thickens (about 15 minutes). Add coconut, milk, and butter. Cook for 4 minutes. Remove from double boiler and cool. Spread over cupcakes or between layers of cake, and sprinkle heavily with coconut.

GAYLORD'S CHEESECAKE (YOUR CHOICE)

1 prepared graham-cracker-crumb shell
3 eggs
1 cup sugar
1 tsp vanilla
2 8 oz pks of Philadelphia cream cheese

Cream sugar and eggs. Add cream cheese and vanilla. Beat well until fluffy. Place in prepared pie crust shell. Bake at 350° for 23 to 27 minutes. Cool.

TOPPING: 1 pint sour cream, 1 1/2 tsp sugar, 1 tsp vanilla. Mix well. Spread topping on cheese cake and place back the4 in oven for exactly 7 minutes. Cool and refrigerate overnight.

To make it your choice, add any of the following fruit toppings: cherries, strawberries raspberries, or blueberries. Yours could be: a strawberry cheesecake, a cherry cheesecake, etc.

STANDARD CREOLE POUND CAKE

8 tbsp butter
1 cup vegetable shortening
2 cups sugar
6 eggs
1 tbsp of each: vanilla, lemon, and orange juice
1/2 tsp lime juice
2 cups sifted flour

Pre-heat oven to 350°. Cream sugar, butter, and shortening in mixer. Add eggs one at a time, mixing well after adding each one. Add flavorings and flour and mix well. Pour cake batter into greased and floured pan and bake for 50 - 60 minutes. Cake is done when a toothpick stuck into it comes out clean.

LEMON CREOLE MERINGUE PIE

1 9" baked pie shell
4 tbsp butter
1/2 cup lemon juice
1 tbsp grated lemon rind
7 tbsp corn starch

1 1/2 cups sugar
1/4 tsp salt
1 ½ cup hot water
2 egg yolks, beaten

Cook corn starch, sugar, salt, and water over medium heat, stirring constantly for 4 to 8 minutes or until mixture is thick and clear (translucent). Remove from heat. Add egg yolks. Place on low heat and cook for 6-8 minutes. Add juices, rinds, and butter, and stir until well incorporated. Pour mixture into baked pie shell and top with meringue, made with egg whites with about 1 tsp whipped until fluff.

CREOLE PEANUT BRITTLE

1 tbsp soda
1 tsp vanilla
2 cups raw or roasted peanuts (no salt)
1/2 cup of each: water, sugar, brown sugar, and corn syrup
1/2 stick butter

With raw peanuts, mix or turn until peanuts pop with roasted unsalted peanuts. Add 1 tbsp soda and 1 tsp vanilla. Mix remaining ingredients on low heat. Beat well and pour into buttered pans or on buttered plate or table top.

CREOLE FRUIT CAKE (CHRISTINE PAUL)

1 1/2 lbs. raisins
1 1/2 lbs. almonds
1 1/2 lbs. pecans
1/2 lbs. walnuts
1 lb. butter
1 1/2 lbs. citron, cut fine
1 1/2 lbs. candied pineapple
1 lb. flour, sifted
1 lb. sugar

1 grated nutmegs (do not use pre-ground or others)
1 tbsp vanilla or vanilla extract ,
1/2 pint sherry (or mixed candied fruit: orange, cherry, pineapple, etc.)
6 eggs

Cream butter and sugar well. Add 1 egg at a time. Beat well after adding the sifted flour and then the nutmeg. Pour half of flour over fruits and nuts and blend remaining half of butter mixture, adding sherry, alternating. Add flavoring extracts. Fold in floured fruits and nuts. Line the bottom and sides of a tube pan with paper (parchment or waxed). Cover the top of the cake pan by tying down over the top several thickness of waxed paper or use sheets of aluminum foil. Place the cake pan in a pan of water (about 3" deep on the sides of the pan). Steam. Bake in 275 to 300° oven about 3 1/2 hours. Remove the cover and pan of water. Bake for another 1/2 hour at 325°.

WALNUT, PECAN, PEANUT AND ALMOND FUDGE

3 cups sugar
3 tbsp cocoa
1 small can evaporated milk
1/2 cup white or clear corn syrup
1/4 cup maple syrup
3 1/2 tbsp butter
1/2 cup walnuts
1/2 cup pecans
1/4 cup peanuts
1/2 cup almonds
1 candy thermometer

Mix sugar, cocoa, corn, maple syrup, and milk together and cook over low heat (use a thermometer) until soft ball stage, stirring only 3 to 4 times during cooking process. When fudge reaches soft ball stage, remove from heat. Add butter and let it set until pot is cool enough to touch the bottom. Add walnuts, pecans, peanuts, and almonds. Beat by hand, mixing well. Pour in square pan or on a waxed surface.

BASIC CREOLE ICING

2 1/2 to 3 cups powdered sugar
1/4 cup cream
1/4 cup milk

Combine enough powdered sugar in milk and cream mixture. Mix well until spreadable or leave to a desired degree of thickness. Place in a piping bag or icing dispenser.

POUND CAKE ICING

1/3 cup half and half
3 tbsp lemon rind
4 tbsp lemon juice (fresh or constituted)
1 lb. confectioners' sugar
1 cup butter (soft)
A dash of salt

Cream butter, lemon juice, and lemon rind. Sift sugar well, then add sifted sugar and Half and Half. Spread frosting on pound cake. Place leftover icing in the refrigerator.

OLD FASHION NEW ROADS PECAN CANDY (PRALINES)

1 cup brown sugar
1 cup white granulated sugar
2 cups pecan halves
1/2 cup rich cream or condensed milk
2 1/4 tbsp butter

Dissolve sugar in cream and bring to a boil. Do not scald. Stirring occasionally, add butter and pecans. Cook until the syrup reaches the soft ball stage (about 238-243°). Cool without disturbing. Beat until somewhat thickened but not until the glossiness is gone. Drop by Tbsp onto a well-greased flat surface or waxed paper lined surface. Candy will flatten out (makes about 23 pieces).

FIG PRESERVES

3 1/4 cups sugar
1 1/4 cups water
1 slice lemon or 1 tsp fresh lemon juice
3 quarts figs

Wash figs very well in water. Then, drain them and scald them. Drain well before cooking. Combine sugar and water in large iron pot. Bring to boiling point. Add figs and lemon. Cook slowly about 2 to 2 3/4 hours. Seal in sterilized jars when cool.

CREOLE BROWNIES

1/2 cup almonds, pecans, and walnuts
½ cup peanuts
4 eggs,   2 tsps vanilla
1 cup melted butter and white sugar
1 cup brown sugar
4 heaping tbsp cocoa
1 1/2 cups flour

Mix all ingredients well. Pour mixture into a 14 1/2 x 12 or larger pan and bake at 325° for 30-35 minutes. (Makes 2 dozen brownies.)

Icing:

2 tbsp cocoa, 3 tbsp rum
5 tbsp butter
1 large egg
3/4 box powdered sugar

Mix ingredients well and use to spread on brownies.

CREOLE HOT FUDGE TOPPING

1 1/2 tsps vanilla
3 cups powdered sugar, unsifted
5 squares semi-sweet chocolate
8 tbsp butter
1 large can evaporated milk

Melt chocolate and butter in a double boiler. Remove from heat and add milk, alternating milk and sugar. Bring mixture to a boil over medium heat and cook about 8-10 minutes, until thick and creamy, stirring constantly. Remove from heat and add vanilla. (Makes 2 1/2 to 3 cups.)

A HOST OF FRIENDS

This portion of *How I Learned to Cook Great Creole Food*, from Gram, Pop, and a host of family members, now brings the many FRIENDS I have shared great times with. "Each one teaches one," is a phrase which is self-explanatory. Through the years I have been able to share some of my family's heritage, traditions, and culture with friends. The Creoles were always known as people who shared. Some of them, though, would not give you a recipe, but would give you the food, the reason being, some Creole recipes were strictly kept in the family and only passed on from one generation to the next. Through the years, the strict control of those recipes and family secrets have been passed on to others, in hopes that they would be kept alive. I would like to thank the many friends and their relatives who provided recipes for this section of the cookbook. We all hope everyone will find great pleasure in bringing many of these great recipes to their family's table. In addition, I want you to share these recipes with your family and friends.

RUSSELL MALLET (T-POP'S) ROASTED LEG OF LAMB

6 lb. leg of lamb (lean trimmed)
1 chipotle pepper dried
2 smoked dried jalapeno peppers
2 tsps cumin seed
2 sprigs thyme
1 tsp oregano
1 medium, onions - chopped
2 stalks chopped green onions and celery
Salt and black pepper
Brown, wild, or cinnamon rice

Dry roast thyme, oregano, and cumin seeds together until smoky. Do not burn. Add chipotle and jalapeno peppers and grind well. Pepper and salt lightly the leg of lamb. Smear with olive oil. Coat lamb with herb mixture, onions, and celery. Place in 325° oven for about 45 minutes to 1 hour. Serve roasted leg of lamb with the rice of your choice.

PRESTON ROBERTS CREOLE STUFFING

Olive oil (non virgin)
1/4 cup chopped onions
2-3 cloves garlic (chopped or mashed)
2 lbs. lean ground pork (sauté until dark in color)
1 tsp salt and pepper
2 oz. white dry wine
1/4 cup chopped almonds and raisins
1 tbsp capers
¼ cup fresh pimentos. 1 dash coriander
¼ cup andouille sausage, chopped
1 1/2 cups milk

French bread (soak in milk) or 4 cups non-sweetened corn bread. Combine all ingredients. Place in dish and cover. Bake in oven at 325° for about 35-45 minutes. Let cool. Use to stuff turkey, chicken, etc.

PAUL PICKNEY'S ROAST DUCK

6 ducks
2 medium yellow or red onions
2 tsps chicken bouillon or 1/2 cup chicken broth
2 sprigs parsley
2 stalks celery
¼ lb butter
2 tsp sage
1 12 oz. pack of unseasoned bread crumbs
Creole seasoning and salt and pepper

Combine onions, celery, and parsley with 2 1/2 cups cold water in a blender. Process mixture until fine and pour into a large sauce pan. Add butter, bouillon, or chicken broth. Heat well, until all is mixed together. Stir in bread crumbs and let sit. Save. Wash ducks. Dry well after washing. Spoon bread crumb mixture into duck cavities. (Do not close cavities. Rub outside with Creole seasoning). Place ducks on a rack in baking dish. Roast covered at 325° for 2 1/2 to 3 hours or until tender. Remove cover and turn oven to 450°. Roast until golden brown. Baste with pan dripping during roasting process.

LOUIS BOWMAN'S GLAZED CARROTS

2 lbs. carrots cleaned and cut any way you wish
3 tbsp butter
1/2 tsps sugar
Salt and pepper to taste
Water (enough to cover carrots)
1 tbsp additional butter
1 tsp parsley, finely chopped

Pre-heat oven to 325°. Place carrots and other ingredients in baking dish. Bake from 45 minutes to 1 hour or until carrots are soft and tender. Drizzle with honey.

ROBLEY BRUNO'S ASPARAGUS WITH LEMON-TARRAGON BUTTER

2 tbsp Butter
1 tsp chopped fresh tarragon
1/2 tsp grated lemon peel
1/2 tsp lemon juice
1 15 oz. can asparagus spears, drained, or
1 bunch of fresh asparagus

In a small sauce pan, melt butter. Stir in tarragon, lemon peel, and juice. Simmer 2 to 2 1/2 minutes over low heat. Pour over warmed asparagus spears. If you use fresh asparaqus, blanch or par boil . Use cold water to stop cooking process. Then add sauce.

NETTIE BROWN'S CRANBERRY SAUCE

1 lb. fresh cranberries or 1 large can
2 cups granulated sugar
1 tsp finely grated lime zest
1 tsp finely grated orange zest
1 tsp finely grated lemon zest
1/4 cup fresh lime juice
1/4 cup fresh lemon juice
1/4 cup fresh orange juice
1/4 cup water
2 8oz. packages of Philadelphia Cream Cheese

Combine all ingredients in heavy sauce pan. Bring to boil, reduce heat to medium/low, and simmer 10 minutes until berries pop open. Skim foam off surface. Cool to room temperature and add packages of cream cheese (room temperature). Refrigerate. Place in a mold to make a great presentation. When ready to serve, remove from refrigerator.

JAMES EAGLIN'S BASTING SAUCE

1 stick butter
2 - 4 tbsp honey
1/2 cup sherry wine
1/2 cup fresh orange juice (frozen is okay)
Cheese cloth

Heat all ingredients in pan. Let cool. Place sauce on cheese cloth. Place cheese cloth over turkey, ham, chicken, etc.)

AARON WASHINGTON'S CREOLE SAUSAGE STUFFING

12 cups cornbread, cut into 1" cubes
4 tbsp olive oil
5 tsps dried thyme
2 lbs. turkey sausage (remove casings)
3 cups chopped onions
6 ribs celery, chopped fine
1 cup dried cherries or cranberries
2 tbsp chopped fresh sage or
2 tsps dried sage
1/4 cup chopped parsley
2 cups chicken broth
Salt and freshly ground black pepper (or red)

Preheat oven to 350°. Place cubes of corn bread in bowl with 2 tbsp olive oil, 2 tsps thyme, salt, and pepper. Toss well and lay out on 2 baking sheets. Bake for 15 minutes or until toasted slightly. Return to bowl. Cook sausage in nonstick skillet over medium/high heat until thoroughly cooked, breaking up the meat. Brown lightly. Remove and add corn bread, breaking it up. Place remaining olive oil in sauce pan. Cook onions and celery for 10 minutes over medium/low heat, stirring. Add cherries or cranberries. Cook for 5 minutes. Spoon mixture into cornbread. Toss remaining thyme, sage, and parsley with corn bread to moisten, 1/2 cup at a time, until moist to individual liking. Adjust seasoning to taste. Cool to room temperature.

(If using turkey or duck, do not stuff the night before roasting). To prepare stuffing inside turkey or duck, bake at 350° to 400° for 1 to 2 hours until bird is golden brown.

AL DONATA'S POTATO DILL BISCUITS

2 cups all-purpose flour
2 tbsp baking powder
1/2 tsp baking soda
1/2 tsp salt
1 tsp dried dill

2 tsps dill seed
3/4 cup skimmed milk
1 tbsp melted butter
1 tbsp sugar
1 1/4 cups mashed potatoes

Preheat oven to 425°. In a mixing bowl, whisk together all dry ingredients. Set aside for a moment. In another mixing bowl, add butter, milk, and potatoes. Use an electric mixer until all nice and smooth. Stir in dry ingredients. Drop large tbsp of mixture onto a lightly greased cookie sheet. Place in oven until lightly brown or golden brown.

MILDRED CARRIERE'S CREOLE GARLIC SOUP

2 tbsp grated Parmesan cheese
1/4 cup softened butter
4 slices French bread
1 cup dry sherry wine
2 cups water
2 10 oz. cans of beef broth or consomme
4 to 8 large cloves of peeled garlic

Add garlic cloves to beef broth in sauce pan and simmer for 15 minutes or until garlic is soft. Remove garlic and save until later. Add water and sherry to broth and continue the heating process. Toast French bread on one side. Then spread on un-toasted side with butter. Mash the garlic that was saved earlier and spread it over the French bread. Sprinkle with cheese. Broil toast until cheese bubbles. Place toasted French bread in soup bowl, ladle hot soup over bread, and serve.

Gaylord Boyd was a finalist in the Carla Hall Presents "MY FAVORITE CHEF" competition recently conducted by the Food Network, coming in third among 100 favorite cooks and bakers from many nations:

https://favchef.com/2025/gaylord-boyd

He is also featured in the Chef John Folse cookbook created in conjunction with the Cardiovascular Institute of the South, *Something Old & Something New: Family Recipes from the Past and Made Heart Healthy Today*. This cookbook combines the best of both worlds. It features 200 traditional Louisiana Cajun and Creole recipes, along with a healthier, modified version.

In this day and age of diets and health food, this book offers great alternatives to some of Louisiana's best recipes and features more than 200 pages of color photos and family stories associated with the original recipes. This cookbook is considered a must-have for all food enthusiasts.

ORDER BLANKS

Copies of the cookbook can be sent anywhere.
They make great gifts or a nice reference book for yourself.

Send money order payable to G. Boyd:
916 Mayflower Street
Baton Rouge, LA 70802-6322

Each cookbook $20.00 Shipping & Handling $9.95
Total $29.95

Also available Holiday/Any Occasion Gift Baskets.
Email (grasshopperink1@gmail.com) or call (225) 270-5777
for additional information.

Send Book (s) To:

NAME: _____

ADDRESS: _____

CITY: _____

STATE: _____

ZIP CODE: _____

www.ingramcontent.com/pod-product-compliance
Lightning Source LLC
Chambersburg PA
CBHW040304170426
43194CB00021B/2894